Animal Babies

Mammals

Rod Theodorou

Heinemann Library
Chicago, Illinois

Customer Service 1-888-454-2279
Visit our website at www.heinemannlibrary.com

Text designed by Celia Floyd
Illustrations by Alan Fraser
Printed in China

04
10 9 8 7 6 5 4

The Library of Congress has cataloged the hardcover version of this book as follows:
Library of Congress Cataloging-in-Publication Data
Theodorou, Rod.
    Mammals / Rod Theodorou.
        p. cm. – (Animal babies)
    Includes bibliographical references and index.
    Summary: Introduces the birth, development, care, feeding, and characteristics of baby mammals.
    ISBN 1-57572-883-4 (lib. bdg.)
    1. Mammals—Infancy—Juvenile literature. 2. Parental behavior in animals—Juvenile literature. [1. Mammals. 2. Animals—Infancy. 3. Parental behavior in animals.] I. Title. II. Series: Animal babies (Des Plaines, Ill.)
    QL706.2.T48 1999
    599.13'9—dc21   99-17397
                            CIP

Paperback ISBN 1-57572-544-4

Acknowledgments
The Publishers would like to thank the following for permission to reproduce photographs:

BBC/Andrew Cooper, p. 10; John Cancalosi, p. 15; Anup Shah, p. 17; Thomas D. Mangelsen, p. 23; Carl Englander, p. 24; Bruce Coleman, p. 21; Mark Carwardine, p. 5; Jane Burton, p. 6; Rod Williams, p. 13; Frank Lane/Silvestris, p. 11; NHPA/A.N.T., p. 7; E. A. Janes, p.12; Gerard Lacz, p. 22; Michael Leach, p. 26; OSF/Richard Kolar, p. 8; Martyn Colbeck, p. 16; Owen Newman, p. 19; Mike Birkhead, p. 20; Mark Deeble & Victoria Stone, p. 25; Tony Stone/Renee Lynn, p. 9; Art Wolfe, p. 14; Norbert Wu, p. 18.

Cover photo: Oxford Scientific Films/Konrad Wothe

Some words in this book are in bold, **like this**. You can find out what they mean by looking in the glossary.

Contents

Introduction

There are many different kinds of animals. All animals have babies. They take care of their babies in different ways.

These are the six main animal groups.

Mammal   Bird   Reptile

Amphibian   Fish   Insect

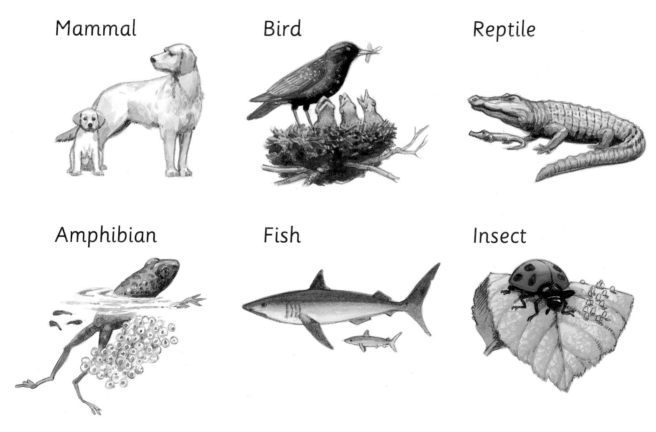

This book is about mammals. Mammals live all over the world. Some mammals are tiny. Some mammals are huge.

The biggest mammals in the world are blue whales. An adult can be longer than a basketball court.

What Is a Mammal?

All mammals:
- breathe air
- get milk from their mother's body
- have hair on their bodies

Dog

hair

Most mammals:
- grow babies inside the mother's body
- give birth to live babies
- live on land and walk on four legs

Platypus babies **hatch** from eggs, but they are mammals, too!

Birth

Some mammal mothers have one baby at a time. Others have lots of babies at once. Most mammals look for a safe place to have their babies.

Mice can have more than fifteen babies in one **litter**.

Some mammal babies are born blind. Their parents take care of them until their eyes open. Other mammal babies can see and run with their parents very soon after they are born.

The mother orangutan carries her baby
on her back until it can take care of itself.

Taking Care of Baby

Most mammals take care of their babies. Small mammals build burrows or nests for them to live in. They bring them food until they are old enough to find their own.

This mother fox has dug a burrow in the ground to keep her babies safe and warm.

Some mammals have to keep moving to find food or keep out of danger. Some carry their babies by the **scruff** of the neck. Other babies hold onto their mothers.

This baby bat holds onto its mother even when she is flying.

Feeding

Mother mammals feed their babies milk from their bodies. The milk is very rich and helps the babies grow quickly.

The babies nearest this mother pig's head get the best milk.

Mammals need lots of food for **energy** and warmth. As the babies get older, their mothers **wean** them off milk. The babies have to start eating solid food.

These snow leopard babies are waiting for their mother to bring them meat.

Moving Around

Some mammal babies can move around soon after they are born. They learn to walk or run so they can escape from **predators** and follow their parents.

Baby giraffes have to stand up and run soon after they are born.

Other mammal babies cannot walk or run when they are born. They stay close to their mother while they grow bigger and stronger.

Joeys leave their mother's **pouch** when they are about nine months old, but they jump back in if they are scared or hungry.

Family Life

Many mammals live in large family groups, called **herds**. They help each other look after the young and **protect** them from danger.

When the herd goes to look for food, some female elephants stay behind to baby-sit all the young elephants.

Mothers in a herd always know which babies are theirs by their look, smell, and call. They spend a lot of time **grooming** and cleaning their babies.

Chimpanzee mothers pick dirt and insects out of their babies' hair.

Brothers and Sisters

When they are young, most mammals spend a lot of time with their **siblings**, especially if they live in a **herd** or family group.

Young dolphins swim with their siblings. They may even fight and bully young dolphins from other families or groups.

Brothers and sisters sometimes have play fights. This helps them grow stronger. It is also good practice for fighting **predators** or for hunting **prey**.

This game will help these lion cubs learn to hunt and catch food.

Learning from Parents

Some mammal babies have very good **instincts**. They do not have to learn everything from their parents. They know how to find food and look out for danger.

A young mouse knows how to find food and stay hidden from **predators**.

Other mammals have to learn some things from their parents. Some remember how their mothers took care of them, so they can look after their own babies.

Whale calves can swim as soon as they are born, but their mother has to push them to the surface to teach them to breathe air.

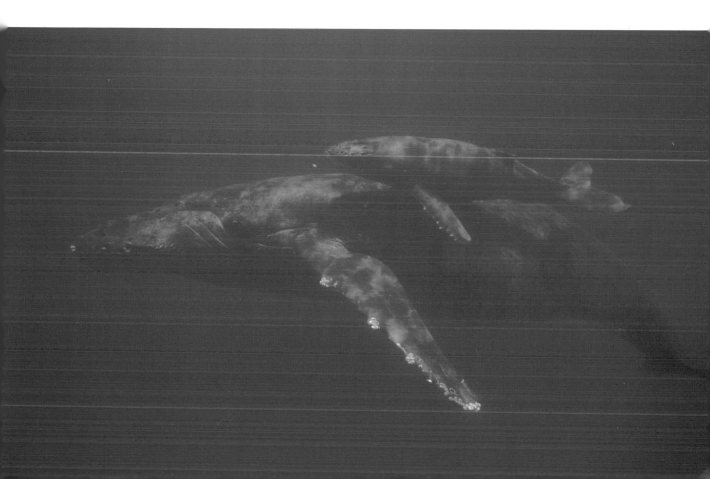

Learning to Feed

Many mammals teach their babies to hunt or find food. Hunting mammals sometimes bring small or **injured** animals back to their young so they can learn how to kill.

This tiger mother teaches her cubs how to hunt other animals.

Some baby mammals spend a lot of time watching how their mother finds food. They will remember what plants are good to eat or what animals are easy to catch.

These bear cubs watch carefully to see how their mother catches fish.

23

Staying Safe

Most mammals try to **protect** their babies from danger. They may call to their babies if a hunter is near. The babies stand near their parents or run to a safe place.

When musk oxen are attacked by wolves, the big adult oxen stand in a circle with their babies safe in the middle.

Some mammals are camouflaged. This means the color of their skin or hair makes them hard for **predators** to see.

These cheetah cubs blend in with the tall grass, so it is hard for predators to see them.

Leaving Home

Some mammal babies take years to grow up. Others grow up very quickly. Once they have grown up, all mammals **mate** to have babies of their own.

Voles are ready to have their own babies when they are only fifteen days old!

When they are old enough, some mammals leave their mother and find a new place to live. Other mammals stay with their family or their **herd** all their lives.

Humans are mammals. We spend more time living with our parents than any other mammal.

		Fish
What they look like:	Bones inside body	all
	Number of legs	none
	Hair on body	none
	Scaly skin	most
	Wings	none
	Feathers	none
Where they live:	Live on land	none
	Live in water	all
How they are born:	Grow babies inside body	some
	Hatch from eggs	most
How babies get food:	Get milk from mother	none
	Parents bring food	none

Amphibians	Insects	Reptiles	Birds	Mammals
all	none	all	all	all
4 or none	6	4 or none	2	2 or 4
none	all	none	none	all
none	none	all	none	few
none	most	none	all	some
none	none	none	all	none
most	most	most	all	most
some	some	some	none	some
few	some	some	none	most
most	most	most	all	few
none	none	none	none	all
none	none	none	most	most

Glossary

energy   to be able and strong enough to run around and play or hunt

groom   to keep healthy by cleaning and brushing fur or hair

hatch   to be born from an egg

herd   large group of animals of one kind that live together

injured   hurt

instinct   to know how to do something without being told how to do it

joey   baby kangaroo

litter   group of animals that are born at the same time and have the same mother

mate   when a male and a female animal come together to make babies

pouch   pocket of skin on the stomach of some animals in which their babies grow

predator   animal that hunts and kills other animals for food

prey   animal that is hunted by another for food

protect   to keep safe

scruff   loose skin at the back of an animal's neck

sibling   brother or sister

wean   when a baby animal stops feeding on its mother's milk and eats other food

More Books to Read

Butterfield, Moira. *Big, Rough, & Wrinkly*. Austin, Tex.: Raintree Steck-Vaughn Publishers, 1997.

—. *Brown, Fierce, & Furry*. Austin, Tex.: Raintree Steck-Vaughn Publishers, 1997.

—. *Fast, Strong, & Striped*. Austin, Tex.: Raintree Steck-Vaughn Publishers, 1997.

Berman, Ruth and Lynn M. Stone. *Fishing Bears*. Minneapolis: Lerner Publishing Group, 1998.

Doudna, Kelly. *Piglets*. Edina, Minn.: ABDO Publishing Company, 1999.

Esbensen, Barbara J. *Baby Whales Drink Milk*. New York: HarperCollins Children's Books, 1994.

Robinson, Claire. *Chimpanzees*. Crystal Lake, Ill.: Heinemann Interactive Library, 1997.

—. *Lions*. Crystal Lake, Ill.: Heinemann Interactive Library, 1997.

—. *Bears*. Crystal Lake, Ill.: Heinemann Interactive Library, 1997.

Index